# KATHARINE HEPBURN

# KATHARINE HEPBURN

## A Life in Pictures

Edited by Pierre-Henri Verlhac
Foreword by Charles Higham

CHRONICLE BOOKS
SAN FRANCISCO

# KATHARINE HEPBURN

Foreword by Charles Higham

"ACTING'S JUST WAITING FOR A CUSTARD PIE. THAT'S ALL." The magnificent Katharine Hepburn's parting words to me, following a meeting to discuss an authorized biography on a chilly, rainy afternoon at her West Hollywood home in 1974, summed up her philosophy of the art that she practiced incomparably for more than seven decades. She saw herself as "a more or less gifted amateur," she told me, who got lucky early on and, with some major bumps along the way, stayed lucky until her old age. Happily, the world has disagreed.

For her, acting was no more than a glorious hobby; Kate saw herself as the least important member of an antic Connecticut family that included her father, a successful surgeon, her mother, an activist feminist, a sister who prospered as a New England farmer, another sister who married well, and a brother who wrote plays. Nobody was as surprised as she was when she won, in her twenties, an Oscar for her performance as the eager, desperate young actor Eva Lovelace adrift in New York in *Morning Glory*, or in her maturity, as Christina Drayton, the liberal wife who finds her daughter about to marry an African American in *Guess Who's Coming to Dinner*, and a third time, as the fiery twelfth-century royal matriarch Eleanor of Aquitaine in *The Lion in Winter*. It was only the last of these movies that pleased her totally; but she underrated her performance even in that film, crediting whatever merit it had to the director, her friend Anthony Harvey.

Many famous people acknowledged her worth when she did not. Writing of her stage performance in Shaw's *The Millionairess* in 1952, Kenneth Tynan said, "She glows like a branding iron, and marks you her willing bond-slave." Writing of her in *The Philadelphia Story*, Brooks Atkinson averred, "There are no ambiguous corners in this character portrayal. Dainty in style, it is free and alive in its daring expression of feeling." Sir David Lean, who directed her in *Summertime*, told me that working with her was like "bottling lightning."

Few disagreed; but some found Kate hard to work with. She even usurped the role of art director: On the sets of *Holiday* and *The Philadelphia Story*, she rearranged the furniture and replaced the curtains. On *Guess Who's Coming to Dinner*, she asked for a fake fireplace to be removed. When she made *The Lion in Winter*, she insisted on the accuracy of twelfth-century clothes and sets, when a week before she knew nothing about them; her speed-reading of historical texts had made her an expert, and a real one.

While as an exponent of the art of acting she saw herself as overrated, Kate had no time for the alternatives to a stage and screen career: marriage and children. Her marital union with the Philadelphia socialite Ogden Ludlow Smith was a disaster; she ended it after three weeks, when he told her to do the washing up. As for children, "What," she asked me, "would I have done with them when I was acting . . . chain them up in the yard?"

She never went to drama school, taking lessons instead from an old-fashioned coach, Frances Robinson-Duff, who taught her all the wrong things: the back of the hand to the forehead to express grief, a damp handkerchief fluttering from fingers in farewell. She intruded personal feelings into rehearsals: When she was working with the notorious Broadway director Jed Harris on *The Lake*, Harris told her to jump in it. She ran up to him during rehearsal, embraced him, and said, "I have loved you, I love you now and I will always love you." He pushed her away saying, "You haven't acted, you aren't acting now and you will never act." And she had recently won her first Oscar.

Kate's spontaneous expression of emotion, her lack of restrictive technique, and calculated gesture marked her from the first. She could cry more convincingly than any other actor because without any use for Method acting she could recall, when needed, moments in her life of intense grief, and burst rapidly into tears. When I asked her about this, she laughed and said the reason she cried so often was because she had been stricken with conjunctivitis on David Lean's *Summertime*, in which she memorably played a spinster secretary falling in love with a married man in Venice; she had taken a step backward in a scene and fallen into filthy canal water that permanently affected her eyes. I didn't have the temerity to remind her that she had superbly sobbed, in *Alice Adams*, to mention only one movie, many years earlier. Whereas other stars would have flung themselves on a bed to weep, she let the tears fall at a window in full view of the audience.

No mere coach could teach her the art of playing trag-
edy or comedy, at both of which she was a master. In
an unforgettable scene in *Woman of the Year*, as a colum-
nist who, like Kate herself, marries without domestic
skills, she tries to prepare breakfast and drops an egg
on her shoe. She learned that in sequences like this,
to bring laughs, the performer must look as glum as
possible; typecast as a zany Connecticut heiress in the
comedy classic *Bringing Up Baby*, she never telegraphed
the jokes.

Although she wouldn't say it to me, truth was her yard-
stick, and she could detect falsehood in a line immedi-
ately, and have it rewritten, or even rewrite it herself. She
hated "bunk," her favorite word, in people and in pictures. When a director offered her bunk, she responded
quickly: Furious with Joseph L. Mankiewicz, her director
on *Suddenly Last Summer*, in which she played the mother
of a tormented homosexual, she spat in his face in front of
cast and crew.

Kate was an overactive tomboy as a child. Born to that
maverick clan in Hartford, Connecticut in 1909, she, in
living contradiction of her disparagement of her own
acting ability, was on stage almost continuously from
childhood. First in *Bluebeard*, she murdered her "wives"
in a straw beard dyed that color; in *Beauty and the Beast*,
she was a handsome Beast. When she took up figure skat-
ing, she earned a prize at Madison Square Garden. She
played touch football with boys, and jumped fully clothed
into the pool at Bryn Mawr.

She started in shows in New York, demanding parts at
auditions and usually getting them. She announced herself at one audition as coming all the way from Hartford
with a bit between her teeth. She made a splash in a now-
forgotten Broadway play called *The Warrior's Husband*,
striding onto the stage with a stuffed deer slung around
her shoulders. Soon Hollywood noticed her, and she was
summoned to RKO to read for the part of the tortured
daughter of John Barrymore in *A Bill of Divorcement*.
Arriving at the test with two red eyes from cinders on the
train (Barrymore said she had been drinking), she gave
a nervous, mannered performance, but her star quality
was clear. George Cukor, the equally energetic director,
decided to give her a chance.

Barrymore tried to make love to her in his dressing room. Her reply was typical: "My father doesn't want me to make babies." That chilled even his famous lust. Soon she found a lover in the agent Leland Hayward; having him collect her earnings as well as make love to her was a typically smart idea.

Kate's father's investments for her made her rich and independent, even in the Depression, giving her the kind of security that meant that if a producer didn't like her ideas for movies, she could go back to New York, where the real action was. She thought Hollywood society absurd, and once served producer Walter Wanger's dinner party as a maid. Nobody recognized her. She even refused an invitation to Pickfair, Hollywood's Buckingham Palace, presided over by Mary Pickford. ("That was my finest moment," she told me.)

*Morning Glory* was a reflection of herself and spurred Pandro S. Berman, head of RKO, to adapt part after part for her, most notably Jo, the rebellious daughter in *Little Women*, a great triumph for her; and Linda Seton, the spoilt heiress, scion of a Park Avenue family, in *Holiday*.

Kate did well as the pretentious, Shakespeare-spouting, boarding house actor Terry Randall in *Stage Door*, but soon her too-precious vehicles, including *The Little Minister* and *Quality Street*, failed, and movie exhibitors listed her as Box Office Poison.

Racing around Hollywood in expensive cars while wearing slacks, rejoicing in a haunted house which she rented to Boris Karloff, saying she must have left a spark behind when an ocean liner she had sailed in caught fire, Kate was always in the news while avoiding reporters as assiduously as Greta Garbo. Her angular figure, red hair done up in a knot, and flashing face as bright as any on a silver coin ensured many of the striking photographs this book contains.

Some memorable photographs in this book illustrate Kate's work in those rare vehicles in which she stepped entirely outside herself, and the star part wasn't hand-tooled for her. As Mary, Queen of Scots, in John Ford's underrated *Mary of Scotland*, she was unexpectedly convincing as the romantic, impassioned monarch caught up in political intrigue of which she understood little, finally sent to the execution block by a vengeful Queen Elizabeth I. Kate looked superb in her meticulously accurate Stuart costumes and jewelry, which, thanks to her research, drew a memorable, emotionally authentic picture of the doomed queen.

Her one big disappointment was not being cast as Scarlett O'Hara in *Gone with the Wind*: The producer, David O. Selznick, told her he couldn't imagine Rhett Butler chasing her for 12 years. "Some people's idea of sex appeal is different from yours," she snapped, as she strode furiously out of his office.

Kate had an affair with a fellow eccentric, Howard Hughes, who taught her to fly, played golf with her at dawn to avoid the press, had her pack the sandwiches and put ping pong balls in the plane (optimistically) as flotation devices in case it should land in the sea on his record-breaking flight round the world, and she finally lost him because Ginger Rogers beat her to the bedroom (she upset a jug of water on Rogers's head). Hughes helped her to finance *The Philadelphia Story*, which playwright Philip Barry wrote for her; she dazzled as the

spoiled, brittle Pennsylvania heiress on stage and screen; her dash, her fire, her unpredictable charm and bursts of anger, her essential vulnerability, all were portrayed in one of the greatest parts of her career; she was Box Office Poison no more.

Kate had fallen in love with Spencer Tracy long before they met. She told me that she cried when he drowned as a Portuguese fisherman in *Captains Courageous*. Cast opposite him in the political comedy *Woman of the Year*, she was thrilled; but almost sank her chances when, meeting him in a corridor at MGM, she said, "Won't I be a little tall for you?" "Don't worry," Joseph L. Mankiewicz later said, "he'll soon cut you down to size."

Tracy did just that; she let him discipline her as nobody else ever could. He was a handful. Married, Roman Catholic, with a deaf son, he was fussy, melancholy, wry, easily upset—the opposite of his solid, uncomplicated, rugged image onscreen. His alcoholism and resulting poor health turned Kate into a nurse. Unselfish for the first time in her life, she became not only his lover, but his sister, his mother, his lifelong chum. Not even the worst gossips, Hedda Hopper and Louella Parsons, could gripe at their illicit romance. Kate made sure of that from the beginning, sending Hedda Hopper a Christmas card painting of a nose and advising her to keep hers out of other people's business. She also had her boss Louis B. Mayer silence Louella on the matter. Sometimes fans proved too much for her, as when one stopped her on a New York street and said, "We made you what you are," and she snapped back, "Like hell you did!"

She filmed *The African Queen* away from Tracy, in jungle conditions that had the rest of the cast ill, but saw her out catching butterflies and exploring ants' nests between scenes. She photographed elephants and wild boar head-on and never got trampled. "They wouldn't have dared," director John Huston told me.

After *Summertime*, Kate toured Australia in *Shakespeare*; typically, her chief memory of the trip was watching the dance of the lyrebird in a forest north of Melbourne, which only six people had ever seen. "It was a command performance," she told me with a laugh.

She became a painter on the set of *The Old Man and the Sea*, which Tracy shot without her in Cuba; her beautiful watercolors of blue ocean and white stone and sails filled a wall of her house in West Hollywood. ("You can say anything you like about my acting," she growled as I stood admiring them, "but don't criticize my painting." I wouldn't and couldn't.)

Her greatest performance was as Mary Tyrone, the tortured, morphine-addicted wife of the former stage star played by Sir Ralph Richardson in Sidney Lumet's screen version of the Eugene O'Neill play *Long Day's Journey into Night*. No actor who substituted technique for naked emotion could have acted the part as well; her sufferings with Tracy were there for all to see. In the movie *Guess Who's Coming to Dinner*, it was clear that Tracy was seriously ill, and in this case her crying wasn't always called for by the screenplay. Asked by director Stanley Kramer if she'd like to reshoot a crying scene, she replied that she was suffering from "cannelitis venicianus" and had him keep it in.

Kate didn't turn up for the Academy Award she won for that picture, or for *Morning Glory* or *The Lion in Winter*, but she did appear for her friend and neighbor, the producer Lawrence Weingarten, when he won a special lifetime honor. Dressed in a black Mao suit, she dazzled; what she wouldn't do for herself, she did for a pal. Needless to say she was given a standing ovation.

She was a smash as Coco Chanel in *Coco* on Broadway. Director Michael Bennett told me had a surefire way of having her, say, exit left. He told her to exit right.

The Uris Theater was being built at the time. It was close to the Mark Hellinger, where she was performing in the show. Matinées were made intolerable by the noise of drilling. One afternoon she had had enough. To the audience's delight, she stopped in the middle of a song, strode out through the stage door, crossed to the Uris, took a workman's elevator to the top girder, walked on it in high heels, and harangued the foreman. When she returned, the audience stood and cheered. She continued the song as if nothing had happened. Building on Wednesday and Saturday afternoons stopped, delaying the Uris's completion.

Kate went on working into her eighties, chiefly to help filmmakers make deals, but in pictures that were unworthy of her. Until she succumbed to a coma in the 1990s, she was as active and alive as ever. After her landlord George Cukor increased her rent, she moved first to her home at Turtle Bay, New York City, and then finally settled down at her beloved house at Old Saybrook, near the mouth of the Connecticut River.

Kate maintained her view of acting to the end. "Spence," she told me in one of our last conversations, "always said, 'Learn the lines and get on with it.' Larry Olivier said, 'Don't bump into the furniture.' They were the greatest. I tried to learn from them." And so, spectacularly, she did.

1911 | Katharine Hepburn, age four.

1915 | Young Katharine Hepburn
(far right) with her brothers (from
left to right) Thomas Jr., Richard,
and Robert, and their mother,
Katharine Martha Houghton.

Undated photograph |
Katharine Hepburn
in mid-dive.

Opposite: 1934 |
Hepburn in a publicity
photo for *The Little
Minister*, directed by
Richard Wallace.

14

1932 | Katharine Hepburn and John Barrymore in *A Bill of Divorcement*, directed by George Cukor.

1932 | Publicity photo of Hepburn for the RKO Pictures (Radio-Keith-Orpheum) studio.

1933 | Joan Bennett, Katharine Hepburn, and Frances Dee, three of the four sisters in *Little Women*, an RKO picture by George Cukor.

18

1933 | Joan Bennett, Jean Parker, Katharine Hepburn, and Frances Dee as the four March sisters in George Cukor's *Little Women*.

1933 | Joan Bennett, Spring Byington, Frances Dee, Jean Parker (seated), and Katharine Hepburn sing in a scene from *Little Women*.

1933 | Hepburn and George Cukor in conversation between scenes during the filming of *Little Women*.

Above and opposite: 1933 | Katharine Hepburn in *Christopher Strong*, directed by Dorothy Arzner.

1933 | Katharine Hepburn as a famous female pilot in *Christopher Strong*.

1933 | Hepburn in *Christopher Strong*.

"Life is hard. After all,
it kills you."

Katharine Hepburn

MY·Q-349-A

1933 | Katharine Hepburn and Adolphe Menjou in *Morning Glory*, directed by Lowell Sherman.
Opposite: 1933 | Hepburn and Douglas Fairbanks in *Morning Glory*.

"I think most of the people involved in any art always secretly wonder whether they are really there because they're good or because they're lucky."

Katharine Hepburn

1934 | Promotional photograph of Katharine Hepburn.
Following two pages: Portraits of Hepburn from 1934.

1934 | Katharine Hepburn, draped in a long coat, descends from a United Airlines airplane.

1934 | Hepburn on an airport tarmac.

Opposite: 1935 | Director George Cukor and Katharine Hepburn on the set of *Sylvia Scarlett*.
Above: October 1935 | Hepburn reads the script of *Sylvia Scarlett*.

Promotional photograph for *Sylvia Scarlett*.

1935 | Director George Stevens, Fred Stone, and Katharine Hepburn on the set of the film *Alice Adams*.

"…[Grant's] acting announces what the actresses of the next generation will have: discretion in the effects, perfect timing. [Hepburn] displays a virtuosity akin to that of a great ballet dancer."

George Cukor

1934 | Katharine Hepburn walking in New York City.

Opposite: 1935 | Studio portrait.

1935 | George Cukor and Katharine Hepburn on the set of the film *Sylvia Scarlett*.

1937 | Director Gregory La Cava, Katharine Hepburn, and Adolphe Menjou on the set of *Stage Door*.

1935 | Katharine Hepburn during the filming of *Sylvia Scarlett*.

Opposite: 1936 | Promotional photograph for the film *Mary of Scotland*, directed by John Ford.

"Being a housewife and
a mother is the biggest
job in the world, but if it
doesn't interest you, don't
do it—I would have made
a terrible mother."

Katharine Hepburn

1936 | Katharine Hepburn in *A Woman Rebels*, directed by Mark Sandrich.

Following two pages:
1938 | Katharine Hepburn and Cary Grant practice an acrobatic scene for the film *Holiday*, directed by George Cukor for Columbia Studios.
1938 | Hepburn and Grant in *Holiday*.

Above and opposite: 1938 | Katharine Hepburn and Cary Grant in *Bringing Up Baby*, a film by Howard Hawks.

1938 | Katharine Hepburn and Cary Grant in *Bringing Up Baby*.

# "If you always do what interests you, at least one person is pleased."

Katharine Hepburn

1938 | A portrait of
Katharine Hepburn.

1939 | Katharine Hepburn (bottom) with her sisters, Marion and Margaret Hepburn.

Opposite: March 1940 | Hepburn playing tennis at the Merion Cricket Club near Philadelphia.

1940 | Katharine Hepburn and director George Cukor on the set of *The Philadelphia Story*.
Opposite: 1940 | Hepburn during the filming of the same film.

Opposite: 1940 | Cary Grant, Katharine Hepburn, and James Stewart in a publicity photo for *The Philadelphia Story*.
Above: 1940 | Hepburn in a publicity photo with John Howard, Grant, and Stewart for the same film.

1940 | Hepburn, as Tracy Lord, with her three suitors, Cary Grant, James Stewart, and John Howard, in a publicity photo for *The Philadelphia Story*.

# "Never complain. Never explain."

Katharine Hepburn

1940 | Katharine Hepburn in *The Philadelphia Story*.

1942 | Katharine Hepburn and Spencer Tracy with other cast members in a wedding scene from *Woman of the Year*, a George Stevens film for MGM.
Opposite: 1942 | Hepburn in *Woman of the Year*.

1942 | Katharine Hepburn and Spencer Tracy in the George Stevens film *Keeper of the Flame*.

"Acting is the most minor of gifts. After all, Shirley Temple could do it when she was four."

Katharine Hepburn

1942 | Commemorative photograph taken on the occasion of the twentieth anniversary of the Metro-Goldwyn-Mayer studio (MGM): the president of the studio, Louis B. Mayer, surrounded by sixty-five film stars. In the first row are James Stewart (far left), Lucille Ball (third from left), Katharine Hepburn (to the right of Louis B. Mayer), and Red Skelton (far right). In the second row are Mickey Rooney (fourth from left), Spencer Tracy (behind Louis B. Mayer), and Robert Taylor. Van Johnson is in the third row (behind Spencer Tracy). Also present are Greer Garson, Jean-Pierre Aumont, Walter Pidgeon, and many others.

"I have had twenty years
of perfect companionship
with a man among men.
He is a rock and a protection.
I have never regretted it."

Katharine Hepburn

Undated photograph of Katharine Hepburn having drinks with actor Clark Gable.

1946 | Hepburn and director Vincente Minnelli during the filming of *Undercurrent*.

1947 | Katharine Hepburn during the filming of *The Sea of Grass*, by Elia Kazan.

Opposite: Hepburn on a film set around 1947.

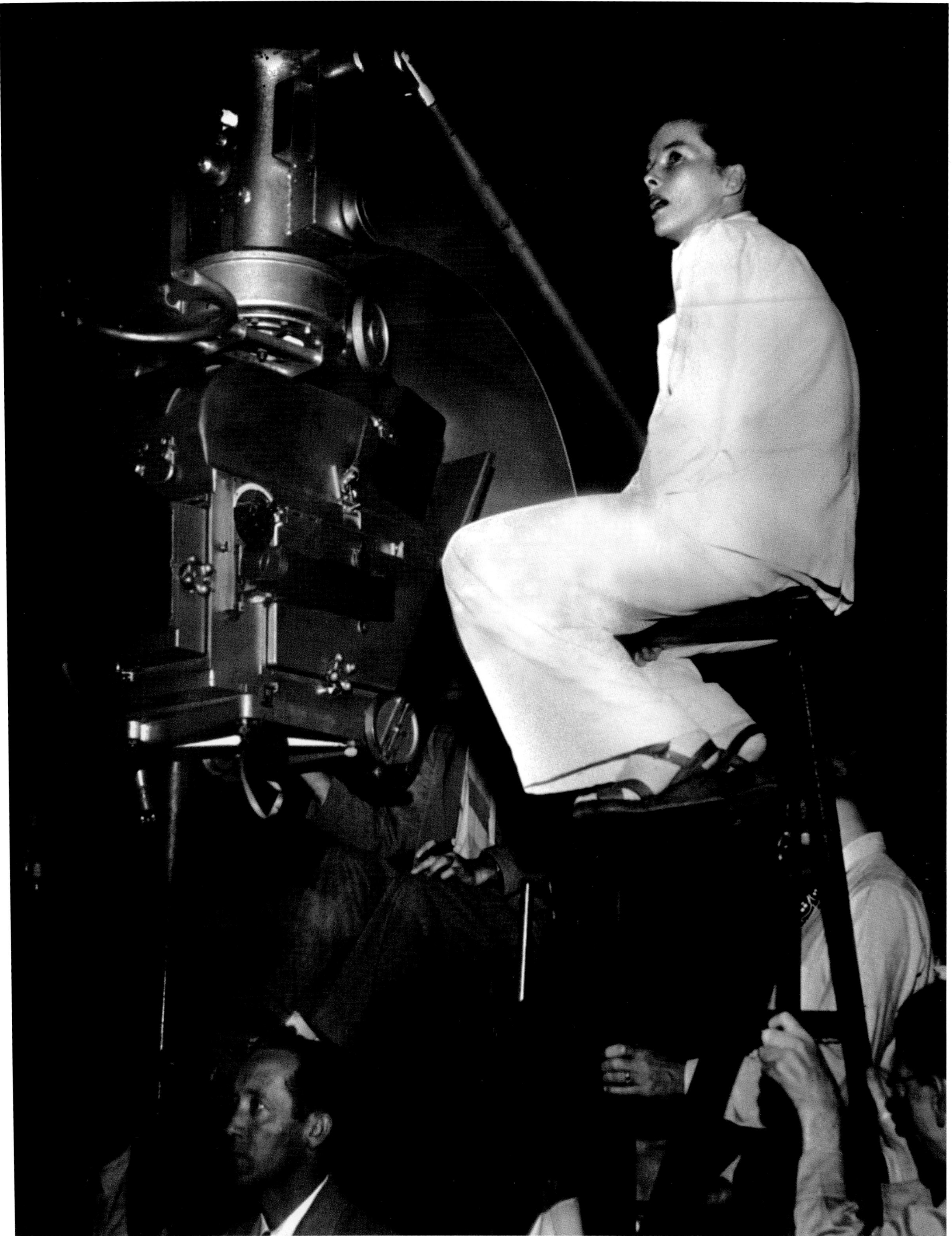

1947 | Katharine Hepburn and Paul Henreid in *Song of Love*, directed by Clarence Brown.
Opposite: 1947 | Hepburn during the filming of *The Sea of Grass*.

"I never lose sight
of the fact that
just being is fun."

Katharine Hepburn

1949 | Katharine Hepburn on the set of *Adam's Rib*.

Following two pages:
1949 | Director George Cukor and Katharine Hepburn on the set of *Adam's Rib*; Tracy and Hepburn in the same film.

1949 | Katharine Hepburn and Spencer Tracy in *Adam's Rib*.

"There is nothing phony about her.… She's really fascinating with a tremendous off-beat kind of sex appeal which throws out a challenge that not any hunk of man can take up."

Humphrey Bogart

1951 | Humphrey Bogart and Katharine Hepburn in John Huston's *The African Queen*.

1951 | Movie poster for
*The African Queen*.

Opposite: 1951 | Hepburn in
*The African Queen*.

AFRICAN QU

1951 | Lauren Bacall, Humphrey Bogart, and Katharine Hepburn.

1951 | Hepburn and Bogart in
*The African Queen*.

Opposite: 1952 | Katharine Hepburn practices playing tennis for her role in *Pat and Mike*, a film by George Cukor, costarring Spencer Tracy.
Above: 1952 | Aldo Ray, Tracy, and Hepburn in a scene from *Pat and Mike*.

"As an actress, she's a joy to work with. She's in there trying every minute. There isn't anything passive about her; she 'gives.' And as a person, she's real."

Cary Grant

DELI3MARTIRI
A SCUOLA DEI FABRI

1956 | Katharine Hepburn and Burt Lancaster in *The Rainmaker*, directed by Joseph Anthony.

1956 | Left and this page:
Hepburn during
the filming of
*The Rainmaker*.

“I never realized until lately that women were supposed to be the inferior sex.”

Katharine Hepburn

1957 | Katharine Hepburn and Barbara Hall at the Theater Festival in Stratford, Connecticut. Hall was auditioning with director John Houseman, while Hepburn had roles in two Shakespeare plays, *The Merchant of Venice* and *Much Ado About Nothing*.

1956 | Hepburn with film crew, including costume designer Johnny Hilling, right, during the filming of *The Iron Petticoat*, a movie directed by Ralph Thomas and costarring Bob Hope.

1956 | Portrait of Katharine Hepburn.

Opposite: 1959 | Katharine
Hepburn on the set of
*Suddenly, Last Summer*,
a film directed by Joseph L.
Mankiewicz.

Right: 1959 | Hepburn posing
on the set of *Suddenly, Last
Summer*.

"Kate is the most inspiring person I have ever met…. [she has] intelligence that has to do with beauty, grace, and just damned good thinking."

George Stevens

1959 | Katharine Hepburn and Montgomery Clift
on the set of *Suddenly, Last Summer*.

"The average Hollywood film star's ambition is to be admired by an American, courted by an Italian, married to an Englishman, and have a French boyfriend."

Katharine Hepburn

1960 | Katharine Hepburn and Robert Ryan rehearse a scene from *Antony and Cleopatra* at the American Shakespeare Festival Theatre.

Following two pages:
1959 | Hepburn converses with a member of the crew on the set of *Suddenly, Last Summer*.
1962 | Hepburn in *Long Day's Journey Into Night*, a film directed by Sidney Lumet and costarring Ralph Richardson.

NOTICE
PLEASE KEEP THESE
DOORS CLOSED
STAGE BEING HEATED
FOR COMPANY SHOOTING

"Love has nothing to do with what you are expecting to get—only with what you are expecting to give—which is everything."

Katharine Hepburn

1962 | Hepburn in *Long Day's Journey Into Night*.

ADIES ROOM

Left and following pages:
1962 | Katharine Hepburn during the filming of *Long Day's Journey Into Night*.

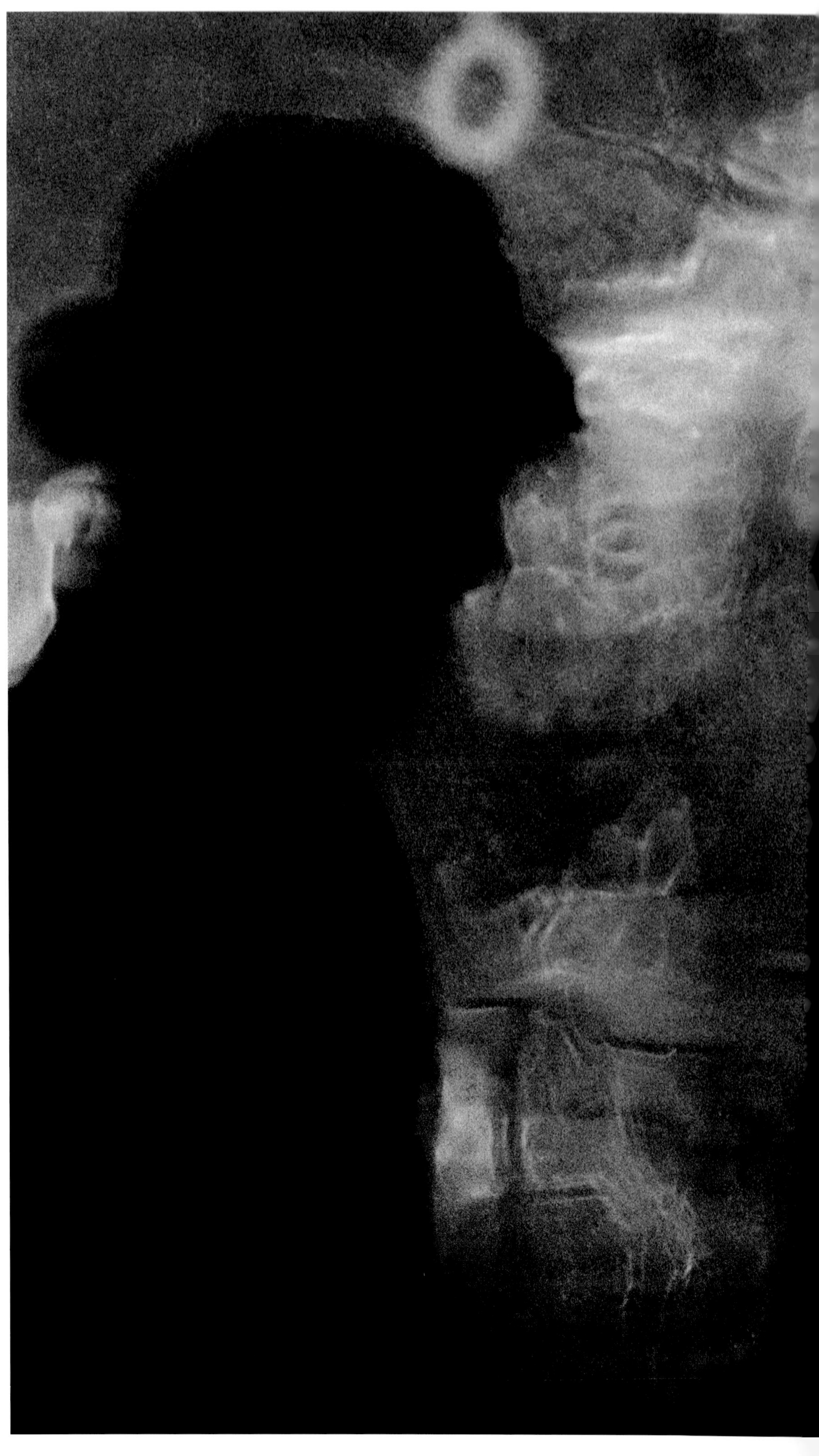

1962 | Katharine Hepburn and Sidney Lumet in the makeup room during the filming of *Long Day's Journey Into Night*.

1962 | Hepburn lost in thought during the filming of *Long Day's Journey Into Night*.

1962 | Hepburn in costume for *Long Day's Journey Into Night*.

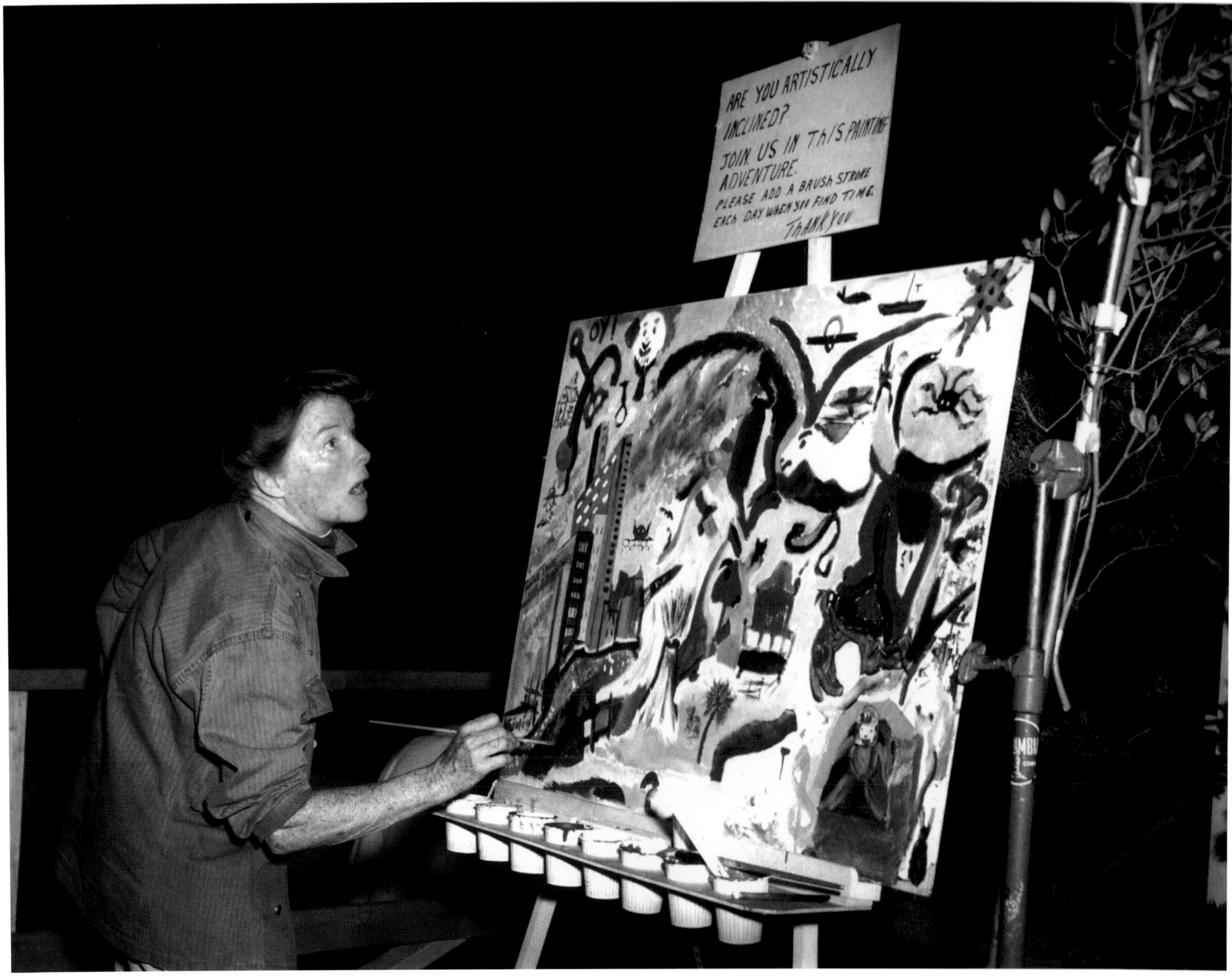


1967 | Katharine Hepburn participing in a collective painting on the set of *Guess Who's Coming to Dinner*, directed by Stanley Kramer and costarring Spencer Tracy and Sidney Poitier.
Opposite: 1967 | Tracy and Hepburn on the set of *Guess Who's Coming to Dinner*.

1967 | Katharine Hepburn and Spencer Tracy during the filming of *Guess Who's Coming to Dinner*.

1967 | Katharine Houghton and Hepburn on the set of *Guess Who's Coming to Dinner*.

# "Time with her was more than time well spent. A little bit with her was worth days and weeks and months with somebody else."

Lauren Bacall

©CPC-GD-

Opposite: 1967 | Katharine Hepburn on the set of *Guess Who's Coming to Dinner*.
Above: April 1968 | Hepburn is congratulated by director Bryan Forbes while filming *The Madwoman of Chaillot* in Nice, France, on learning that she has won her second Oscar for Best Actress for her role in *Guess Who's Coming to Dinner*.

1968 | Portrait of Katharine
Hepburn outdoors.

1968 | Hepburn during the filming of *The Lion in Winter*, a film by Anthony Harvey, which also starred Peter O'Toole, Anthony Hopkins, and Timothy Dalton.

1968 | Katharine Hepburn and Peter O'Toole share a laugh in London during the filming of *The Lion in Winter*.

1968 | Hepburn and O'Toole
rehearse a scene from
*The Lion in Winter*.

1968 | Hepburn in a scene with
O'Toole during the filming of
*The Lion in Winter*.

LEE

1968 | Katharine Hepburn and Peter O'Toole wearing personalized jackets on the set of *The Lion in Winter* with director Anthony Harvey.

1968 | Both pages: Hepburn during the filming of *The Lion in Winter*.

1969 | Katharine Hepburn plays
Coco Chanel in a costume by Cecil
Beaton in the Broadway musical
comedy *Coco*.

1969 | Hepburn as Coco
Chanel in *Coco*.

1968 | Katharine Hepburn
laughing with Danny Kaye during
the filming of *The Madwoman
of Chaillot*, directed by Bryan
Forbes, in Nice, France.

Opposite: 1969 | Hepburn in
*The Madwoman of Chaillot*.

"If you want to give up the
admiration of thousands
of men for the criticism of
one, go ahead, get married."

Katharine Hepburn

1969 | Hepburn at her home
in New York.

1971 | Katharine Hepburn in conversation with Jean-Pierre Cassel in Paris during the opening of the film *The Trojan Women*, directed by Mihalis Kakogiannis, in which Hepburn plays Hecuba alongside Geneviève Bujold, Vanessa Redgrave, and Irene Papas.

1971 | Hepburn with Alain Delon in Paris during the opening of *The Trojan Women*.

"With all the opportunities I had, I could have done more. And if I'd done more, I could have been quite remarkable."

Katharine Hepburn

1971 | Hepburn in Paris during the
opening of *The Trojan Women*.

1974 | John Wayne and Katharine Hepburn with crew during the filming of *Rooster Cogburn*, directed by Stuart Millar.

1974 | Hepburn on the set of *Rooster Cogburn*.

Left and opposite:
1974 | John Wayne and Hepburn
on the set of *Rooster Cogburn*.

Above and right: May, 1978 | Katharine Hepburn speaks during an evening at the Avery Fisher Hall in New York City organized to honor director George Cukor, who had just turned seventy-eight.

1981 | Director Mark Rydell and Katharine Hepburn during the filming of *On Golden Pond*, costarring Jane Fonda and Henry Fonda.

1981 | Jane Fonda, Henry Fonda, and Hepburn during the filming of *On Golden Pond*.

Shoe forms of famous actresses, including Katharine Hepburn (second from top), at Ferragamo, the Italian fashion house.

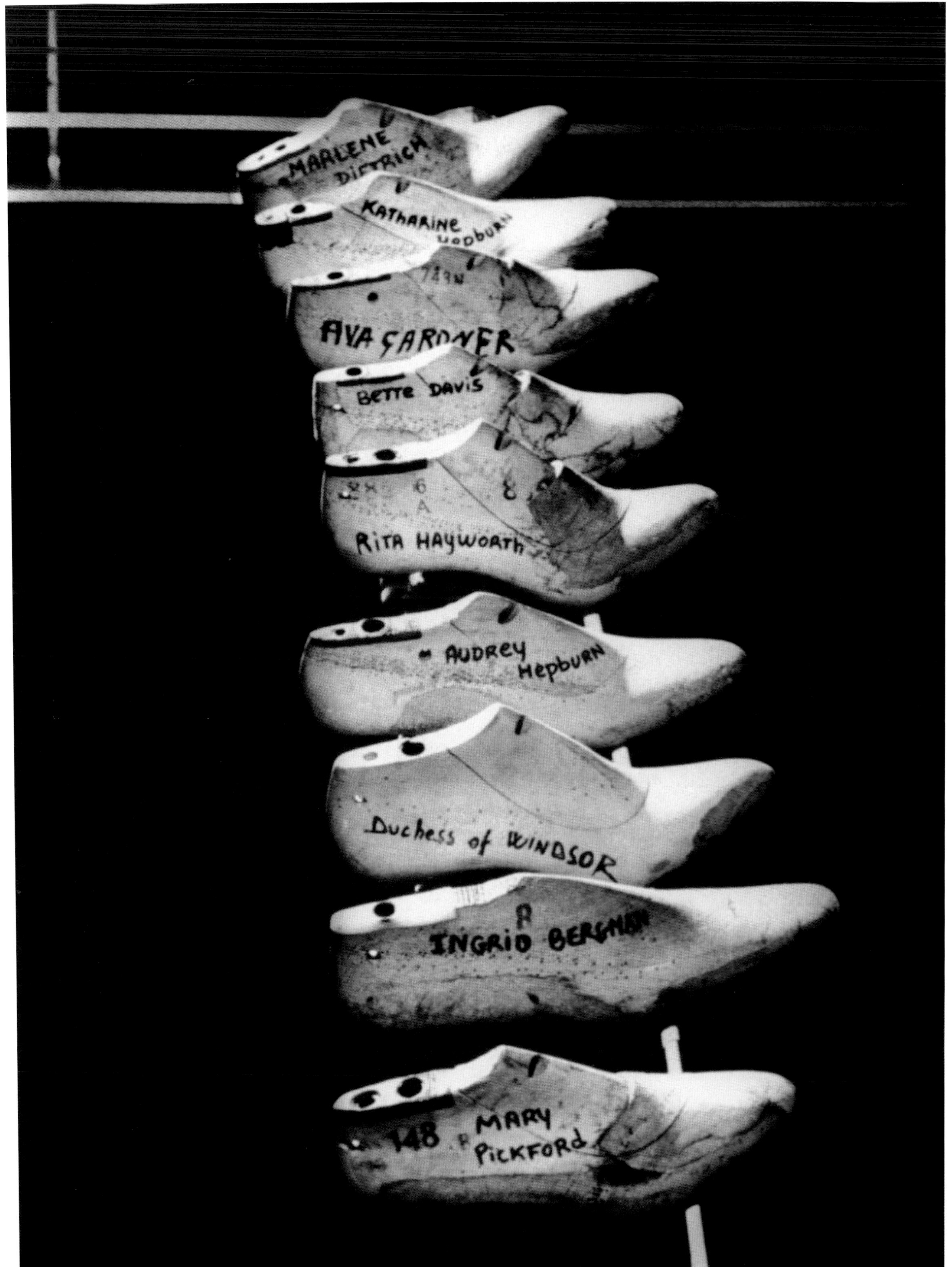

MARLENE DIETRICH
KATHARINE HEPBURN
AVA GARDNER
BETTE DAVIS
RITA HAYWORTH
AUDREY HEPBURN
Duchess of WINDSOR
INGRID BERGMAN
MARY PICKFORD

1980s | Katharine Hepburn out for a stroll in New York City.

1986 | Frank Sinatra introduces Katharine Hepburn at a gala in celebration of Spencer Tracy (1900–67) at the Majestic Theater in New York City.
Opposite: 1986 | Hepburn in the documentary film *The Spencer Tracy Legacy: A Tribute by Katharine Hepburn*.

1990 | Katharine Hepburn picks flowers in the
fields that surround her house in Connecticut.

1990 | Hepburn with jazz musician Dizzy Gillespie during a reception at the White House.

May 1992 | Hepburn arrives at the Waldorf Astoria Hotel in New York.

# "Death will be a great relief. No more interviews."

Katharine Hepburn

1995 | Hepburn reads her mail in her living room.

# Photo Credits

12 | Rue des Archives / BCA / CSU

13 | Rue des Archives / BCA

14 | Collection ChristopheL

15 | Collection ChristopheL

16 | Bettmann / Corbis

17 | MPTV

18 | MPTV

19 | MPTV

20 | Collection ChristopheL

21 | Bettmann / Corbis

22 | Collection ChristopheL

23 | MPTV

24 | MPTV

25 | Rue des Archives / BCA

27 | Collection ChristopheL

28 | Roger-Viollet

29 | Ullstein Bild / Roger-Viollet

31 | Ullstein Bild / Roger-Viollet

32 | MPTV

33 | MPTV

34 | Condé Nast Archive / Corbis

35 | Condé Nast Archive / Corbis

36 | Bettmann / Corbis

37 | Rue des Archives / BCA

38 | Collection ChristopheL

39 | Rue des Archives / BCA

41 | Collection ChristopheL

42 | MPTV

43 | Rue des Archives / BCA

44 | Rue des Archives / AGIP

45 | Rue des Archives / BCA

46 | Sunset Boulevard / Corbis

47 | MPTV

49 | Collection ChristopheL

50 | Getty Images

51 | Collection ChristopheL

52 | Collection ChristopheL

53 | Collection ChristopheL

55 | Collection ChristopheL

57 | MPTV

58 | Rue des Archives / BCA

59 | Rue des Archives / BCA

60 | MPTV

61 | MPTV

62 | MPTV

63 | MPTV

64 | Collection ChristopheL

67 | MPTV

68 | MPTV

69 | MPTV

70 | FIA / Rue des Archives

73 | MPTV

75 | Sunset Boulevard / Corbis

76 | AFP

77 | Collection ChristopheL

78 | MPTV

79 | Rue des Archives

80 | Collection ChristopheL

81 | MPTV

83 | MPTV

84 | Rue des Archives / BCA

85 | Collection ChristopheL

86 | Ullstein Bild / Roger-Viollet

89 | Popperfoto/Getty Images

90 | Collection ChristopheL

91 | Collection ChristopheL

92 | Ullstein Bild / Roger-Viollet

94 | MPTV

95 | Everett Collection / Rue des Archives

96 | Collection ChristopheL

97 | Collection ChristopheL

98 | Bettmann / Corbis

99 | Collection ChristopheL

101 | Bettmann / Corbis

102 | Rue des Archives / BCA

Every effort was made to ascertain the copyright holder of the photographs reproduced in this book. Any errors were unintended by Éditions Verlhac /Chronicle Books and will be corrected in the next print run.

103 | Collection ChristopheL

104 | Ullstein Bild / Roger-Viollet

105 | Ullstein Bild / Roger-Viollet

106 | Ullstein Bild / Roger-Viollet

107 | Bill Avery / MPTV

109 | Rue des Archives / BCA / CSU

110 | Bettmann / Corbis

111 | MPTV

113 | MPTV

114 | MPTV

115 | Burt Glinn / Magnum Photos

117 | Burt Glinn / Magnum Photos

118 | Rue des Archives / BCA

121 | Time & Life Pictures / Getty Images

122 | Rue des Archives

123 | MPTV

125 | Bob Henriques / Magnum Photos

126 | Bob Henriques / Magnum Photos

128 | Dennis Stock / Magnum Photos

129 | Bob Henriques / Magnum Photos

131 | Dennis Stock / Magnum Photos

133 | Dennis Stock / Magnum Photos

134 | Dennis Stock / Magnum Photos

135 | Erich Hartmann / Magnum Photos

137 | Erich Hartmann / Magnum Photos

138 | Rue des Archives / BCA

139 | Rue des Archives / BCA

140 | MPTV

141 | MPTV

143 | MPTV

144 | Rue des Archives / BCA

145 | Bettmann / Corbis

146 | Douglas Kirkland / Corbis

147 | Bob Willoughby / MPTV

148 | Keystone / Eydedea

149 | Bob Willoughby / MPTV

151 | Bob Willoughby / MPTV

152 | Bob Willoughby / MPTV

153 | Bob Willoughby / MPTV

154 | Bob Willoughby / MPTV

155 | Bob Willoughby / MPTV

156 | Bob Willoughby / MPTV

158 | Cecil Beaton / Camera Press / Eyedea

159 | Rue des Archives / BCA

160 | Keystone / Eydedea

161 | MPTV

163 | Bob Willoughby / MPTV

164 | AFP

165 | AFP

167 | AFP

168 | David Sutton / MPTV

169 | David Sutton / MPTV

170 | David Sutton / MPTV

171 | David Sutton / MPTV

172 | Bettmann / Corbis

173 | Bettmann / Corbis

174 | MPTV

175 | MPTV

177 | Time & Life Pictures / Getty Images

178 | Getty Images

180 | Bettmann / Corbis

181 | Rue des Archives / BCA

182 | Time & Life Pictures / Getty Images

184 | AFP

185 | AFP

187 | Cecil Beaton / Camera Press / Eyedea

189 | Time & Life Pictures / Getty Images

First published in the United States in 2009 by Chronicle Books LLC.
First published in France in 2009 by Verlhac Editions.

Copyright © 2009 by Éditions Verlhac.
Foreword copyright © 2008 by Charles Higham.

All rights reserved. No part of this book may be reproduced
in any form without written permission from the publisher.

Library of Congress Cataloging-in-Publication Data available.

ISBN: 978-0-8118-6947-8

Manufactured in China

Translated by A-P-E International
Typeset by Brooke Johnson and Sarah O'Rourke

10 9 8 7 6 5 4 3 2 1

Chronicle Books LLC
680 Second Street
San Francisco, CA 94107

www.chroniclebooks.com